MW01230823

The Highly Unqualified Hand-Guide To Keeping Plants Alive

For my kids...

I know you're "supposed" to listen to your parents

but to be honest

I'm not really sure what I'm talking about,

so just listen to your heart

and be gentle with everyone else's.

Here is my highly unqualified hand guide

to keeping your plants alive.

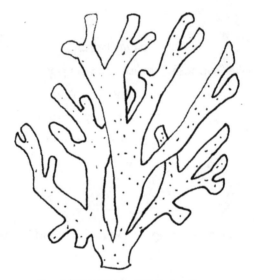

Rich Raun - Cover Design
Megan O'Callaghan - Inside Illustrations
Kyle Dehn - Interior Decorator
Tim Kirch - Overlord

Table of Contents

Water / Sun

Water/Sun/Love/Dirt

Make sure you water them.
But not too much or they'll drown.
Give them plenty of sunlight.
But not too much or they'll burn.
Talk to them often.
But make sure you say the right things.
Keep pests away.
But let the good ones be.
It's all about
Balancing life's contradictions
And navigating through
Every new moral dilemma,
Every last questionable decision,
And determining which type of fertilizer to use.

Start

Where you start is not important.
Starting is the only thing that matters.
The beginning,
The middle,
The end?
Pointless.
If you don't start now
You WILL regret it.
It is scary
But it's never too late
To start anything.
Start a book,
Start learning a new language,
Etc.
And please for the love of all that is holy,
Whatever you decide to start,
Start with the intention of finishing.
Half-ass doesn't look good on anybody.
Ready?
Set...

Endure

There is nothing you can't endure.
I know that sounds like a lot of responsibility,
but it's not.
I know this to be fact
not because I have
successfully conquered every obstacle I've met,
but simply because
everything just happens.
You'll work yourself up
for the big test,
the big game,
the big day,
and no matter the outcome
of all those big moments
the one constant will remain;
they happen.
They come and go.
Sometimes the things that happen
will suck.
And some things will make you cry with joy.
But you endure
and will always endure,
because things happen
and then they don't.

The Phone Pt. 1

Put down the phone

Go climb a tree.

You'll Never See You

You are the most beautiful thing you'll never see.
Not at least until you're old and wrinkly
And your body aches.
You might run into a mirror,
Even daily,
But you'll never understand your beauty.
Just trust me,
I've seen you,
You are stunning.
Flawed?
I hope so.
But don't waste your time worrying about
Your looks,
Because you're the most beautiful thing you'll never see.

Weed Rose

There is
no difference between
a weed
and
a rose.
They start out
as seeds
and
change as they grow.
Why can't both be beautiful?

Always

Whatever
you
do,
allow it
to
fulfill
you
always.

What Was

Don't get too tangled up in the what-was.
What-was, was.
And what will be
Has yet to happen.
Now is the thing.
Actually, it's the only thing.
You can't go backwards and change the past.
You can't jump forward and rearrange the future.
Now is all you have,
So have it fully.
Have it all to yourself.
And share it only
With those
You deem
Worth it.

Internet

The internet
will try to teach you
that it's
not ok to make mistakes,
but life
will teach you
that it's
the only way we grow.

Be You Everywhere

Be yourself.
Unashamedly,
Unapologetically,
Courageously,
Without pause,
Or reservation,
And without the fear of offending,
But don't be callous.
Be you.
When you're alone,
Or surrounded by strangers.
Be you.
In the grocery store,
At the beach,
Or in your car at 3 in the morning.
Be yourself.
Everywhere.
All the time.
Even when you don't feel like yourself
Or even when you don't want to.
Because at the end of the day
No one can be you like you can,
And that makes you the most valuable thing there is.

Dear You

Dear you,
Don't take me in excess
Take what you need
And leave the rest for the others.

Sincerely,

Too Much

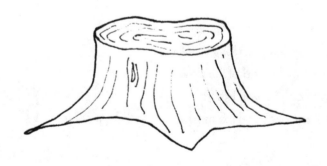

Live Once

How would you live if
nothing happened
after you died?
No glowing ascension,
no dreamy clouds,
no pearl gates,
just nothing.
Impossible-to-comprehend
impossible-to-explain
nothing.
What if,
for a while,
you set your
faith aside
and lived like
you were on fire.
Like being on fire
was a matter
of life or death
here on Earth.
What if
I told you
you are on fire
as we speak
and nothing
happens
after you're put out?

Drama

It's either
going to be
alright
or it isn't,
SO
STOP
WITH
ALL
THE
DRAMATICS.

Vegetables

Try not to stare
Stand up straight
Hold the door open
Listen carefully
Brush your tongue
Look at the clouds
Practice compassion
Most things in moderation
Read books
Speak loudly
Clean your room
Paint pictures
Love feverishly
Hike up that hill
Ignore politicking
Empathy over everything
And yes,
You should probably
Eat vegetables.

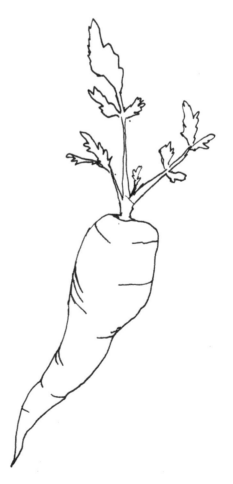

So Simple

It's
so simple
to make
everything seem
so simple,
but
nothing ever is.

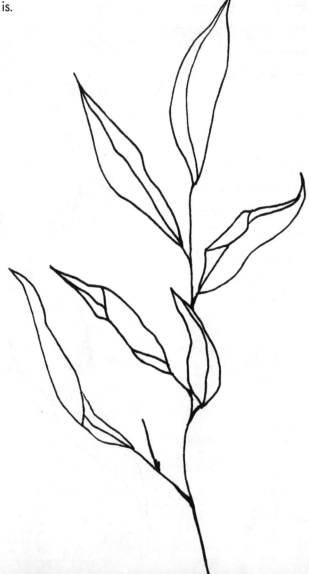

Tail of Time

You can't catch time by the tail.
No matter how hard you try
you will always lose it.
It will always escape you.
You tell yourself,
"I won't let this moment pass me by!"
Then it does
And you say,
"dang."
Pay time little mind at all.
Know that it always
goes by faster than planned,
there's never enough of it,
and by the time
you TRY to make
the most of time
it will already be too late.

Diamonds

Sometimes life will feel
heavy
or constricting
making it seem hard to move
or even breathe,
but
always remember
it takes pressure to make
diamonds.

End / Begin

Something
is ending
in order for
something else
to begin.

Laugh & Cry

Make yourself laugh at least once every day.
A true, bottom of the belly laugh.
At nothing in particular,
or at a dirty joke you read
on the bathroom wall
at a Love's gas station
in Yuma, AZ.
I tend to make myself laugh in the car.
Talking shit to the radio hosts
or screaming along to Madonna.
Laughter has got to be healthy for you,
But I'm no doctor.

And don't be afraid to cry alone.
It doesn't mean you're weak.
And when you cry,
cry like your eyes depend on the water.
The last time I cried
I was watching
a video of your first 7 months here on Earth.
I cried like a baby
while watching my baby.
It felt amazing.
Laugh and cry.
Do them both often.
When you do,
It probably means
you're feeling something.
And by all means,
while you're here,
feel things.

Cheerleader

Avoid envy.
It will only leave you feeling empty.
There will always be
room for more,
but
you have a lot already.
Cherish it.
And for goodness sakes,
be happy for
good people
when good things
happen for them
because
everyone needs a
cheerleader.

Not For Everyone

You don't have to like everyone.
And this may come as a disappointment,
but not everyone will like you.
There is good news though...
you are not for everyone.
You're for those special few
who have lights for eyes
when you walk into a room.
Plus,
it would be
terribly exhausting
trying to be
for everyone.
It's a good thing you're
not for everyone.

Bang

There are some things in life
you weren't meant to understand.
How long do protons live?
Why is ice slippery?
What came before the Big Bang?
No matter how hard you try,
some stuff
won't make sense
which is why gut feelings are important.
A band called The Stills said,
"Logic will break your heart."
And it's true.
Sometimes,
if it makes sense to you,
that's all the sense you need.

Coffee

This is you existing
And not much means more
Not your stress
Not your job
Not your anxiety
This is you existing
And you no longer have to hide
From your scars
From your fear
From your self
This is you existing
And that's all there is.
Everything else?
Cream for the coffee.

The Phone Pt. 2

Put down the phone

Go jump in a river.

Don't Beat Yourself Up

Stop comparing today to the past.
It happened,
move on.
Learn from it,
or avoid it all together,
but shame ain't the right medicine.
If you have to say sorry,
say it.
If you don't feel like it's warranted,
then fuck 'em.
But don't beat yourself up;
it happened,
move on.

March

Joining a march
doesn't make you a martyr.
Because without
understanding,
grace
and compassion,
you're just
another asshole
on a walk.

Tricky Love

Intimate love is tricky.
You can be happy without it,
and you can love without being
happy at all.
The real trick
is finding
someone or something
that makes it
seem easy.
Love will always be tricky,
but loving should
be
anything but.

Don't Say It

Don't say it if it's not true
Don't say it quietly
Don't say it just to say it
Don't say it just to hear it
Don't say it to harm
Don't say it to hide
Don't say it halfway
Don't say it's fine if it's not
Don't say it doesn't matter
If you don't mean it
Don't say it at all.

Questions

Never ask questions
you don't want answers to.
But ask a lot of questions.
And then question the answers.
And question the questions too.

Just Wait

Just wait until you realize
        they're all just as lonely
Just wait until you realize
        they're all making it up
Just wait until you realize
        things aren't so bad
Just wait until you realize
        there's more than money
Just wait until you realize
        how much I love you
Just wait until you realize
        how lucky we actually are
Just wait until you realize
        this is only the beginning

And if you're trying to
        figure out what this is all about
                you'll probably have to just wait.

Silence

Sometimes the silence
Is too loud
So we turn it down;
But sometimes
It's exactly
What we need to hear.

Shame

Never use shame as a teaching tool
You will find that it only creates actors.
Account for stupidity
And allow for missteps
Because if what you're actually looking for
Is real,
Concrete change,
You won't find it
On the shelf
Next to shame.
Change exists
On the shelf
Right next to
Empathy.

Understand?

I used to want
to be
Understood
Now I just want
to be
Loved
And sometimes
Listened to.

Write Things Down

Write things down.
Good thoughts
Bad ideas
Funny sounding words
Grocery lists
Reminders to get dog food
You get the point
Sometimes that's all it takes to make you feel a little less...
Blah.
All sorts of wild things have transpired because ink fell out of a pen.
Who knows,
You could become a best-selling author,
Or you could just beat yourself in a game of tic tac toe.
Give it a shot.
What do you have to lose?

(Write your answer here below)
(Just kidding)
(Unless you want to)
(Then write it down)

Fine Feelings

Don't be ashamed
Of your hurt
And your pain;
There is a time
And a place
For every feeling.

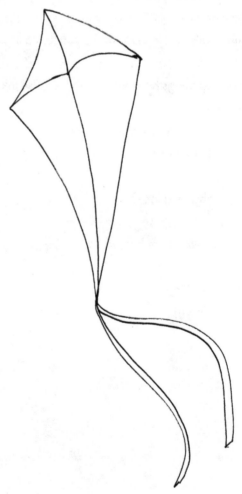

Tough

Everyone gets terrified.
It happens all the time.
But what most people don't realize is,
if you're still here
you possess some special kind of bravery.
You didn't run
or try to escape.
True, life is tough,
but since you're reading this right now
I can tell you with confidence that
you're a tough fucker.
Because to be here
you've got to be brave.
You've been terrified before
and alas, you're still here right now.
So whatever it is you're afraid of
is clearly not as powerful as
the bravery you possess.

Peace

Give me
Peace,
Clarity,
And a
Chance.
Or
Just
Give me
A chance.

Listen

Listen.
Attentively
Incessantly
Compassionately
Like you're the one who's talking
To the wind
And the rain
Listen.
But don't take everything to heart
And 9 times
Out of 10
When someone starts a sentence with
"Listen..."
They'll probably say something
You don't want to hear
But listen anyway
Because
You can always forget
You heard it later.

Am (Not)

I
Am
Strengthened
By all that
I am,
But made
Truly unique
By
All that
I am not.

Full Of It

The older you get,

The more you realize just how full of shit we all are.

Everyone is just making it up

Me

Your mom

All of us

Just trying to cope with the absurdity of existence in our own funny

ways

It's easier pretending to have answers

I hurt less knowing

That everyone gets scared.

But it's ok to hurt

And it's ok to be scared

And it's ok to not have the answers

And it's ok to be full of it.

Beautiful Infinity

Jagged
And bleached,
Crooked-lined,
Chipped-toothed,
Skinned-kneed,
And ugly.
Beauty is
All of these things
too.

For Now

I
Think
I'm
Forever,
But
I'm
Really
Just
For
Now.

Run-On

No matter what your teacher says
Run-on sentences are fine.
Can you imagine how long it took Homer to finish the Iliad?
Have you read it?
I haven't,
But I'm sure there are
Run-ons everywhere.
Breathiness can sometimes lead to a point,
Or can leave you out of breath,
But if what you say is your truth
Don't let the fear of seeing
Some red ink on a paper
Stop you from speaking it.

What You Do

Think little about who you are
And lots about what you do
Because what you do
Is who you are
And who you will be
To anyone you decide
to do anything with.

Age

At 16
I thought I knew it all
Had a car
And a summer job

At 23
I thought I knew it all
Didn't want to be alive
Didn't like myself much

At 30
I thought I knew it all
Happy to be in bed by 10
But happy to be here

Today
I know I don't know it all at all
But I have you
And I have me
And in another 5 years
I hope I know a little more
Than I do now.

Nothing Lost

Nothing beautiful
is ever lost
&
Anything worth anything
will always come
at a cost.

Your Truth

The truth is,
it's hard to find truth.
And maybe the only truth
That actually exists
Is that something only has to
Mean something to you
To mean something at all.

Without Me

You'll survive without me.
Selfishly, I want you to need me.
But you don't.
And though I've given you all I can,
Every last bit of the love in my heart,
You'll get on without me.
And you'll thrive.
I want you to need me,
But at this point I think I need you.
And should you have a little one
Of your own,
You'll understand exactly
What I'm going on about.

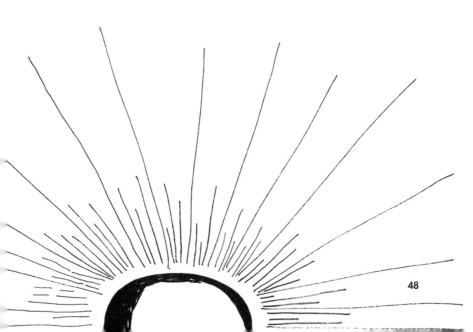

Rental Car

Don't treat life like a rental car.
Sure,
You're bound to get dents
And scratches
Because they're hard to avoid,
But maybe
It's better to treat life like you own it.
Afterall,
It is a limited edition,
1 of 1 model.

Travel From Head To Heart

Take time to travel from your head
Down to your heart
Once in a while.
The road there
Is unpredictable
And you'd think
With all the taxes you pay
They'd fix those
Goddamn potholes along the way
But I think the drive
Will be well worth it.
You see,
Your head is mostly rational.
But sometimes rational needs an antagonist
And when you arrive at your heart,
Listen to what it says,
Drive that same road
Back up to your head,
And tell it what they said.

Quit The News

It's time to quit the news.
Or better yet, don't start watching at all.
Quite literally,
Millions of amazing things happened yesterday,
But you won't hear about them on the evening news.
24 hours in a day.
7.753 billion people in the world.
Surely something incredible happened yesterday?
Not in the news it didn't.
Quit the news.
Go outside.
Put your feet in the grass.
Look up at the moon.
Avoid the excess gloom
And quit the news.
Because amazing is the next breath in,
And the next step you take.

Love / Dirt

Plants

What
does
any of this
have anything
to do
with
plants?

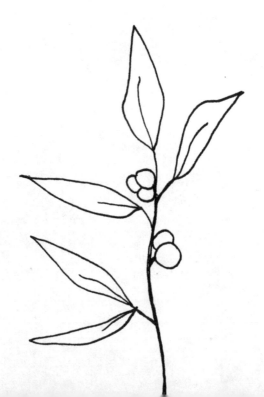

I Love You

I love you
always.
In all ways.
Like
sunbeams
down hallways
in
straight lines,
angled
or
sideways.
I love you
always.
In all ways.

C'est Toi

You Are Stars

There's nothing
Wrong or right
With the stars.
See yourself this way.
Clean palms
And the benefit
Of the doubt.
That's what you get.
There's nothing
Wrong or right
With you.
You are balanced
Perfectly
And you are
Just the way you are.

The Phone Pt. 3

Put down the phone

Go watch the sun set.

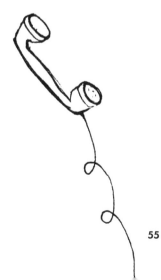

Shaky Bridge

Happiness was a shaky bridge
Between the last time I was sad
And whenever I'd be sad next.
I always made the journey far tougher than it ought to be.
Focused on the worst of things,
The worst was all I got.
Now I try to cross over my sadness
From bright thing to bright thing
Hoping to keep the trouble below.
And although my bridge is still shaky
I know it will hold.

Waiting

No one likes waiting
But how about some patience?
I know you'll get anxious
And start feeling complacent
But don't fill every space with
Something cool-adjacent
Or seek entertainment
By whining in place
Because no one likes waiting
Or the sound of complaining.

Broken Things

Some broken things
can be fixed.
Televisions,
arms,
promises,
accent chairs,
and
hearts,
can all be fixed
with a little
glue,
a couple screws,
and/or
endless amounts of love.

The Joneses

Fuck the Joneses
And keeping up.
It's not a race.
And if it is,
You're racing against you.
Where you are
Is where you are
Not where you'll always be.
Nevermind the pack.
You are in front.
Now keep up with yourself.

The Noise

Step out of the city
Step away from the static
Away from the drive-thrus
And gun smoke
The politics
And daytime tv
It's all so loud
The good noise
Is out
In the wind
Through the trees
In the tiny ripples
Atop forest lakes
In the burning
Embers
Of campfires
And conversation.
Step away from the static
And try listening to the good noise.

Speeds

We all move
At different speeds.
No shame
in the slow lane.
No shame
in the fast one either.
But whatever you do,
don't
get
stuck
on cruise.

Your Tongue

Your tongue
barely weighs
anything at all,
but what you
roll off of it
can weigh more
than most everything else
in this world.

More About Time

I'm not sure time is ever wasted.
I think it's just spent.
Here.
There.
Relaxing.
Panicking.
We don't waste time, we use it.
We mismanage it.
We dismantle it.
We pour it down the drain.
We hold on to it tightly.
Or lightly.
Talk about the old times.
Dream about the new ones.
We can share it with others.
We can keep it to ourselves.
But we couldn't waste it even if we tried.
We spend time.
Now spend it.
Until it's all gone for good.

The Earth

It's not Earth
I'm losing faith in,
It's the humans on it.

Trophy

Not everyone gets a trophy,
But I truly believe
there is a place
for everyone
that doesn't give up.
Giving up is easy.
That's why so many people do it.
The hard part is sticking it out.

Thirty-Something Years

For thirty-something years
I lived a life without you.
Made some friends
Made some mistakes
Won some baseball games
Chipped some teeth
Saw the world a few times over.
I did a lot of living before you,
But could never dream up something like you.
You are worth more
Than all the gold in every sunset
I've ever seen,
And in my thirty-something years here,
And as long as I'm alive,
I never want to know another
Day without you.

Money

Money
Can
Only
Buy
You
Things.

Tomorrow's Problem

It's alright
To sometimes pour the drink
The headache
And regret
And apology thereafter
Can always be tomorrow's problem.

Loyal To A Point

If you find yourself
questioning loyalty,
follow them
to the water
but don't drink
until they prove
they'd follow you too.

Doubt

It's doubtful you'll live
A life without doubt,
But try not to doubt yourself.
I've done the work for you.
I've lost faith in me
So many times now that
I'm qualified to tell you
It's a waste of time.
Save the second guesses
For algebra tests
And game shows.
There are plenty reasons to be a skeptic,
But not a single good one to doubt yourself.

The Day

On
the day
you were
born
the
sky turned
a brighter blue
and
the sun
burned a
warmer red
but
my eyes
had never seen
a shade
like you
on
the day
you were
born.

Same Size Hearts

I am certain
We are all capable
Of loving
And receiving love
Because
No matter the size
We all have hearts.

The Promise

The whole world
could have
crumbled
in a yesterday,
but
there's nothing
quite like
the promise
a today
can bring.

1 vs. 99

The
difference
between
The 1
And
The 99
Is that
The 1
Never gave up.

One Thing

I hope you know
You'll never be
Just one thing...
A student
A carpenter
A daughter
A friend
A jokester
A poet;
You get the point.
You can be all these things
And should be as many things
As you want to be,
Because you're too
Complex
And complicated to be
Just one thing.

I See You

When I see you,
I see you
like I hope
you see you;
green-eyed,
full of life,
and beautiful
in more ways
than you could ever imagine.

Told You

If you couldn't tell by now,
I will tell you a lot of things.
"Wash your face,
go to bed,
mind your manners."
I will tell you a lot of things,
But I'll never tell you
how you feel
and I'll try to never tell you
"I told you so."

Lonely vs. Alone

alone
you will find wonders
for the eyes
inside your head
untangle thoughts of worry
of loneliness and dread
see loneliness
and solitude
are two separate things
loneliness
is lonely
but alone
you will find peace.

Coin Flip

I read something once
About expectations
And how in keeping them low
Or keeping them at bay
You'd somehow ease the sharp blow of reality
Should it decide to set in.
For a while I believed
That this might be a sound
Approach to expectation
But now I think
It's important to expect the most
Out of people and things
Because this place
And these people might deserve
A little blind faith.
At times I've expected peanuts
Only to find a feast.
Don't get me wrong,
My picnic has been rained on
More times than I can count,
But it shouldn't stop me
From planning a picnic.
Life is a coin flip,
So call it in the air
And have faith that
No matter how it lands
Expect the outcome
To be anything but boring.

The Phone Pt. 4

Put down the phone

Close the computer

Turn off the TV

And go outside.

Why Don't You?

Why don't you?   Speak your mind

Why don't you?   Take your time

Why don't you?   Take a chance

Why don't you?   Take a breath

Why don't you?   Take a trip

Why don't you?   See the world

Why don't you?   Spend your money

Why don't you?   Expand your vocabulary

Why don't you?   Make some friends

Why don't you?   Make some mistakes

Why don't you?   Make a wish

Why don't you?   Have a party

Why don't you?   Cry your heart out

Why don't you?   Find some love

Why don't you?   Find someone you need

Why don't you?   Go for a drive

Why don't you?   Nevermind the map

Why don't you?   Ask one simple question

Why don't you?

Been There

I've gone
Where both sunlight and joy
Fear to go
Seconds away
From the end of the world
It's unrealistic
To tell you not to go there
Because sometimes
It isn't up to us
All I'm saying is
I've been there
So should you find yourself there
Know that you're not the first
And you won't be the last
And you most certainly
Are not there alone.

Get On With It

You gave me the gift
Of getting on with it
So I'm getting on with it
And I'm gonna handle it
Carefully and alone
Because before you were here
I was a wreck
And all spun out
But somehow when you came home
Every eye twitch
And shaky hand
Seemed to calm
Enough so that I could get over it
Now I'm getting on with it.
And I'm gonna handle it.

No Suffering

I refuse to believe
We are here to suffer.
It's easier on the heart
To pretend we are here
To love
And cry
All the same...
With every bit of ourselves
That we have to offer.

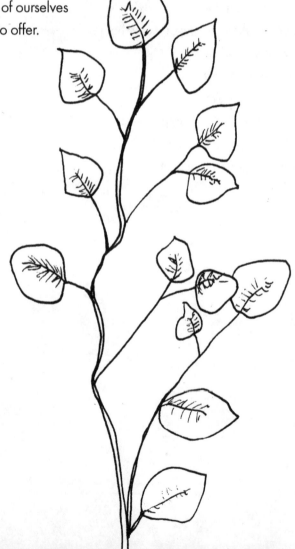

Innocence

People
and this place
will make you doubt
that there's any left;
but it's there.
In the
tiny bubbles
dancing inside your glass
and
in the smells of
gardenia blooms,
gasoline
and
freshly-cut
grass.
No matter how
tightly you grip
it will loosen
and
you'll lose it
but not entirely.
It will come
back to you
in the most
peculiar of faces
and places
and sounds.
I know
you fear you've
lost your innocence
but it's still
there somewhere;
perhaps buried
in the background.

Pretty Things

It's just a
matter of time
until
we're all replaced
by prettier things.
Luckily for us,
pretty is pretty goddamn subjective.
All that said...
I'm certain that
nothing can replace you
because you're the most
objectively beautiful
thing
that eyes
will ever see.

New Logic

The new logic will
tell you to
subscribe here
work faster
eat keto
update your software
"trust us,"
but don't forget
that up until 400 years ago
we thought
the Sun
revolved
around
the Earth.

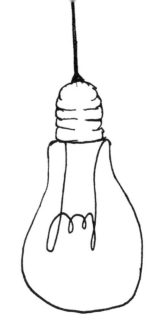

The Comment Section

comments only
mean something if you read them.
so don't read them,
because they don't mean anything.

No One Else

Nothing

Can

Stop

You

But

Yourself.

New Problems

Running away from
your problems
only creates
new problems.
The only way
around them
is through.
Heart open.
Head on.
It may cost a lot,
but it will be worth
a whole lot more.

Sotto Voce

Loud mouths
Don't mean more,
They're just louder.
A soft voice
Can still be heard
And can often have
More to say
Than the loud mouths.
And you may never be
Able to out-loud them,
So let the loud ones
Lose themselves
To hoarseness,
And scratchiness,
And anger
Until they are barely audible.
Then it will finally be
Quiet enough
For your soft voice to be heard.

Thoughts I Have While Lying In Bed

Are the doors all locked?

Is the oven off?

Do we have any eggs in the fridge?

Did I offend him?

How much caffeine is ok?

Can I ever be happy?

Where does Brian Eno live?

What happens to our old batteries?

Should I buy that plaid t-shirt?

Am I a good father?

Will it rain on Saturday?

Which mezcal should I put on the wet bar?

When is labor day?

Why did I waste my time with that person?

Who will be at my funeral?

Could this be the end?

Would you wake up if I turned the tv on?

Can't we just slow down?

Whose voice was on that commercial?

Were the first humans on earth ever anxious?

Does anyone else think about any of this?

Day Job

Just a thought,

but if
your day job
ruins
your day
it's probably best
you find
work elsewhere.

Funny How

Ain't it funny how
I never needed you until now?
Ain't it funny how
You make life easier somehow?
Ain't it funny how
I didn't know
Before you
I was bleeding
I can breathe again
Now that all my walls
Have fallen down.

Ain't it funny how it all works out?

Words & Action

If you say
you're gonna do something,
then do it.
It's hard to build trust with
broken promises
or empty threats.
Because you have your words,
your actions,
and your name.
And if you're untrue
with the first two,
then the last one won't
mean much at all.

The Mood I'm In

I'm sorry
If I've been
Unapproachable
Or I seem
Too emotional
Life as of late has been
A rollercoaster
(So it goes...)
I've been
Avoiding
Confrontational
Bullshit conversations so
If I forgot to say hello
Or if I haven't called back
Just know I've been
Working on this record non stop
I have a baby girl
And a mortgage
And I know they sound like
First world gripes
But I've got em
And I'm not asking you
To solve them
But at least
You now know
That it's all just
A function of
The mood I'm currently in.

Pause Button

There is no pause button
Though right now
I'd push it if I could.
Some moments flee
Like teardrops
On small rocks
In Death Valley in August
And I pay them little mind.
But some moments
Like this one I'm in
Lost in your
Emerald eyes
And that little
Sleepy smile
At sunrise
On some generic Tuesday
In the kitchen...
Moments like these
I wish I could pause and
Stay in all year.

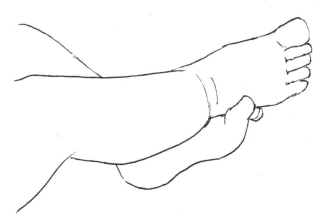

Higher Dose

First breath
Out of a coma
Over and over
Oh what a lovely view of you
A
Two step
Into disorder
I stumble forward
Towards something so brand new.

See
You are something spiritual
Giving me life
Giving me love
Like a second chance
And a second dose.

Dots On Maps

I don't have a plan
But I've got your hand
And we don't need a grand
Just some dots on maps,
An open road,
Our sweaty palms
And a tank of gas.

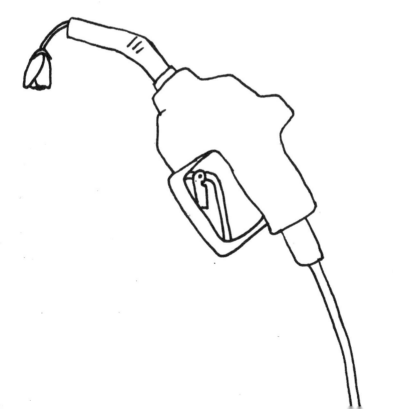

Waiting

Waited all night

Waited all year

Little did I know

I've waited all my life

For you to appear.

Yours To...

Time is
Yours to waste
Secrets are
Yours to keep
Love is
Yours to take
Reality is
Yours to create
Stories are
Yours to share
Scars are
Yours to collect
Hands are
Yours to hold
Hearts are
Yours to break
(but please try not to break them).

Do What You Need To

A decade and a half or so ago
My eyes were shown
Something they could not unsee.
A world which was separate from
The monotonous patterns walked
By somewhere around
96% of the population
(roughly if I had to guess).
It's hard to articulate
Just how infinite the possibilities are
Here on earth.
But by accident
I've lifted the curtain
And seen how many directions
The big wheel can actually spin.
Along the way
Some will tell you
That in order to succeed
You must toe a certain line,
But I urge you to ignore
Both them
And the lines
And walk wherever your feet may take you.

Love Sleeps

Hate
is
never
      more awake

than
when
      love sleeps.

Not First

I don't want
      To be first
            In the world

I just want
      To be first
            In your heart.

Possibilities

i. it's going to be ok

ii. it's not going to be ok

iii. it's ok, then it isn't, then it is, then it's over.

Lux Life

No one needs reminding
that this
overcrowded
polluted
and violent
world is a mess.

All we need
is a
sunset
sunrise
or a love song
to remind us
that life is a luxury
you can only live
not purchase.

Last Thing

This is the end
of my rant
at least in written form
and though
I've advised
you to question most everything
please never question
the following...

I'll
        love you
                until eternity
and then

I'll
        love you
                even more after that.